Beach Walks and God Talks

Diary of a Cowrie Shell

All words and images by
KAREN MARIE ELLISON

KARMEL CREATIONS
Kailua-Kona, Hawaii

Since the creation of the world, God's invisible qualities—His eternal power and divine nature—have been clearly seen, being understood from what has been made. ~ Romans 1:20 NIV

Beach Walks and God Talks
Diary of a Cowrie Shell

ISBN_978-1-735472-80-5
Library of Congress Control Number: 2020914009

KARMEL CREATIONS
Kailua–Kona, Hawaii
beachwalksandgodtalks.com

Printed in the United States of America

For Don

Ink

Aloha fellow treasure hunter,

Will you join me on a journey of discovery along the shores of Hawai'i?

While we walk and talk, we'll cross over lava fields leaving our footprints on the sandy shores of the land, *'aina**. Frequently, we'll walk in silence…basking in the majesty of creation and listening as the Holy Spirit whispers to our hearts. At other times, we'll applaud our amazing discoveries of both the sea and the soul.

There will be a certain magic to our time together. God will be our invisible but clearly heard guide. We'll talk to Him about every little detail of our lives, and He will respond to us as only the Creator of our souls is able.

Cowrie shells are a tiny part of our world. But as we seek out these small shells, we'll be collecting more than just trinkets. We'll unearth treasures of truth that God shows us along the way. Sometimes, we'll uncover, overturn, and recover what has been buried.

Whatever the finds, you can be sure of an amazing adventure…because the riches found in the journey always lead us closer to our final destination.

Are you ready to begin our adventure?

*Hawaiian words that are italicized after the commas can be found in the
Hawaiian glossary at the back of the book.

Treasures

Cowrie ~

Special,

Unlike any other

Sea snail or treasured jewel of the sea?

Common shell or bounty of the beach?

Cowrie, sent special delivery to me.

What is a Cowrie Shell?

A cowrie shell is the external skeleton of a snail-like mollusk that lives and grows within this protective shelter. The diversely decorated ovals are rounded on top and can be identified by a single long and toothy opening on their undersides called apertures.

The name *cowrie* (also spelled *cowry* or *kauri*) originated in India as early as AD 900. Prized for many reasons, cowrie shells have been used over the centuries as money, for trade, in art and jewelry, as religious symbols, and in personal collections. In ancient Hawai'i, cowries were used as bait to lure sharks. They are still used today to catch octopus.

Their scientific name, *cypraea*, originates from the Latin word for the island of Cyprus, where metal was mined to create money. The first coins minted in the classical world were in the shape of cowrie shells. During China's Han period, pottery drums were made to store cowries, and they have been found in Oriental tombs as early as 3,500 years ago. In the eighteenth century, an African bride could be bought for 20,000 cowries.

More than 250 species of cowries are found in tropical waters across the globe, adorned in various colors and patterns. These motifs develop through a rhythmic growth process influenced by their living conditions. Each unique design is not only beautiful but functional—as it serves to camouflage them from their few predators—usually octopus and cone shells.

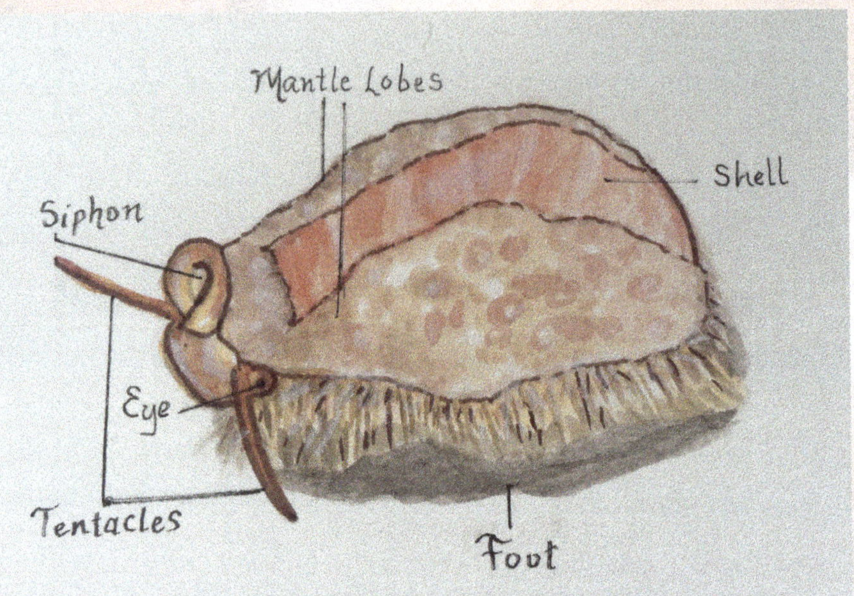

Hawai'i is blessed with at least twenty-five of these species. About ten of them are endemic to the islands. They are more common some years than others, depending on how the currents carry larvae to the shores.

Most cowries live under rocks or coral. They graze nocturnally across the ocean floor, feeding on algae, sponges, and dead sea life. As they move, their shells are covered by a part of their soft bodies called the mantle that extends out from their apertures. This natural process helps burnish them to a natural gloss.

Some cowrie species live as mated pairs. Mom spends several days hidden beneath rocks or in protected depressions with her foot over her larvae. They are born without the protection of their shells. Shortly after birth, their shells begin developing.

Many species live in the same small area for their entire lives. Larger cowries live up to ten years, while smaller ones live two or three years.

It is these vacated shelters that I seek as I walk and talk to the Creator of them and us.

Like people, cowries are essentially the same creatures within, no matter what their exteriors look like. We are all vulnerable beings created to give God glory.

Diary of a Cowrie Shell

I love beach combing.

At this junction of land and sea, I heartily breathe in the mingled smells of salt and sand. Turquoise skies and sapphire waters greet one another on the distant horizon. It is here that I find peace. I come here often in the early morning, to prepare myself for the new day...and my spirit is set free with *ha* (the breath of life).

The beach in front of my home is bordered by a hedge of black explosive lava, *ʻaʻa*. This age-old guardian of the land seems to whisper, "Protect this *ʻaina*. Find rest in this age-old sanctuary." It is at this place that I feel *Hawaiʻi nei* (love for the land).

White sand beaches and palm-tree-lined coves meander through the lava, reflecting the land's ancient heritages. Almost every microclimate of the world from hot deserts to snowcapped mountains converge here.

As I stroll the beach each morning, the aquamarine swirl of ocean reaches out for my toes, then evenly retreats into its vast depths, leaving maritime gifts behind on the waiting shore. Cowrie shells, corals, pebbles, and sea glass are unearthed from their hiding places. I pick up a few of them along my path.

I love cowrie shells.

I found my first cowrie shell, *leho*, glistening in the soft Hawaiian sand when I was nine years old. Instantly captivated by the sea-polished oval glistening in the afternoon sun, I tucked the treasure in my small palm, feeling as if I'd uncovered hidden treasure.

I love finding treasure.

There are so many treasures to be found—gifts of the sea that drift silently ashore to be rescued by those who admire their beauty. Some are partially buried, and I take the time to uncover them, revealing the fullness of their artistry.

I love hearing from God.

But the time I spend meandering the shoreline isn't just spent gathering trinkets from the sea, *kai*. My search for cowrie shells brings me quiet times to converse with God. I reflect on who He is and hear His voice whispering to me in the depths of my soul. It is some of these treasures I share with you in this book.

"Daddy, here I am. What treasures do You have for me today?"

Morning at the Shore

Seek first the kingdom of God and his righteousness,
and all these things will be added to you. ~ Matthew 6:33 ESV

Hawai'i's land, *'aina*, overflows with God's artistry. My senses awaken with the breath of morning when the sweet scent of plumeria flowers joins the rhythmic beating of waves upon the shore – rising in unison to greet me. The blending blues of sky, *lani*, and sea draw me to the beach, ready to receive all the new day, *la*, has to offer.

I come seeking treasures from the sea and treasures for my heart. My Father, Abba, teaches me many lessons as my feet sink sweetly into the soft sand or tread carefully across the rough lava, *'a'a*. Both cowrie shells and a sense of God's presence can be found as I search for them with open eyes and listening ears.

With my mind focused on Christ, I receive the words God is waiting to speak to me. The soft voice of the Holy Spirit often inspires me with a biblical truth through some trinket of His creation. It could be a shell, a rock, or a fragment of sea glass. In these quiet times of searching, I learn lessons I would otherwise miss in the busyness of daily life.

I always come home renewed after my walks. Even on days when I don't find cowries, God provides the food of inspiration for my day. There is no greater treasure than knowing God is there to walk and talk with me every day.

Today's Treasure

Take time to seek God in your day and you will find Him.

When do you plan time to meet with God during your day?

Teach me, Lord.
I wait, Lord, for You,
Your child is waiting.
Teach me to wait.
Speak, Lord, to me,
Your child is listening.
Teach me to listen.
Open my eyes.
Open my ears.
Open my heart.
Here am I, Lord.
"I AM here."

7

New Every Morning

O Lord, in the morning you hear my voice;
in the morning I prepare a sacrifice for you and watch. ~ Psalm 5:3

Like the tideline that is dressed in a fresh marine medley every morning, each new day is filled with its own set of affairs that needs to be sorted out and prioritized. Deciding where to focus is easier when I've discussed it with the One Who Knows. I can't tackle every issue, just as I can't take home every shell I find on the beach, so I need God's wisdom when making decisions.

I come to the beach filled with the expectation that God will meet me here. It's not that I must come to the shore to pray, *pule*, with my heavenly Father. In fact, I pour out my thoughts and prayers to Him all day long. But it is here that I listen the best. I know He hears me wherever I am, but sometimes I get too busy to hear Him.

For me, the beach is a special place to eat my spiritual breakfast. I receive the daily bread of His Word and drink the water of His Spirit. Time spent walking in His creation nourishes my hungry heart. And when I leave the beach, *kahakai*, I surrender my day to God, taking His peace as my gift...along with any cowries He sends my way.

Just as the sunrise backdrops are created uniquely fresh each morning, God makes each day new. I can trust Him to help me through each one of them from sunrise, *pukana la*, to sunset, *napo'o la*.

Today's Treasure

God is always ready to converse with you.
Where do you hear the voice of God the clearest?

Waxy Cowrie

Cypraea cernica Sowerby

Ranging from one half inch to one and a half inches in length, this rare cowrie lives beneath small clumps of coral in waters over sixty feet deep.

Talents Shared Are Talents Earned

His master said to him, "Well done, good and faithful servant. You have been faithful over a little;
I will set you over much. Enter into the joy of your master." ~ Matthew 25:21

Jamie is an artist who creates shell art and sells it at the local flea market. When we talk, it is like two children, *keiki*, at a birthday party. She shares about each of her cowrie pieces with intimate detail, even recalling where she found each shell—most near her home about 40 miles from my own. When she invited me over, I didn't hesitate to accept her invitation.

What I didn't expect to find when I arrived was a sort of shell museum. She greeted me outside on her carefully pieced together patio floor, where the mosaic of cowries and other ocean whatnots was remarkable. Stepping inside, I was astonished by the collection of original furniture, lamps, bowls, and even cooking utensils crafted from her finds. I found my favorite feature of all in the backyard—a shower lined with varied patterns of inlaid shells. The only part of the shower that wasn't embellished with sea treasures was the ceiling…because there wasn't one! Only God's beautiful sky!

When I considered the years she had devoted to collecting, planning, and placing each piece in its perfect spot, I was reminded of the parable of the ten talents. Jesus tells the story of three servants who are given talents (money) to manage for their master. When the master later checks his accounts, he finds two of the servants have invested their talents wisely, and he rewards them for their faithfulness.

The third servant thought the safest thing to do was bury the talent, so it couldn't be stolen. When the master finds out that no profit was made on his investment, he takes the servant's talent from him and gives it to the one who made the best investment.

While the talents mentioned in Scripture speak of money, the same principle can be applied to our God-given abilities. Our heavenly Father gives each of us a certain number of talents to work with. Like muscles, these talents atrophy if they aren't used regularly. On the other hand, they become more powerful when they are faithfully exercised. Both the effort and discipline are pleasing to our Master.

Jamie's commitment to using her talents inspires me to use my gifts wisely. The choice to share or hide our talents is ours to make. We are God's hands here on earth to bring glory to His Name.

Today's Treasure

Your talents ~ use them or lose them.

Do you have a talent that could use a bit of nurturing?

Jamie's Outdoor Shower

The Life of a Ligament

From Him the whole body, joined and held together by every supporting ligament, grows and builds itself up in love, as each part does its work. ~ Ephesians 4:16 NIV

Searching for cowries just after sunrise, a small black cone shell catches my eye. At first glance it seems hardly worth noting. The ordinary-looking shell doesn't compare to the shiny cowries I've found elsewhere, and it's not remarkable in any way.

But as I start to pass by this little shell, God's thoughts permeate my mind. I pause as I realize it is just as precious to Him as the cowries I admire so much. This shell serves a purpose and is here for a reason. As part of His creation, God's attention is as much on this cone shell as it is on the lovely "sea star."

We often see certain people in the church as "stars." But the Bible talks about the importance of the whole body of Christ working together as one.

While the faces, hands, feet, and other obvious parts of the body of Christ often get the most attention, let's not overlook the people who work unnoticed behind the scenes. They are vital parts of the body that hold us together. What would we do without all those prayer warriors hidden in their "closets" fighting for us in the heavenlies?

The unseen ligaments in our bodies support our organs, keeping them in their correct places. Ligaments are defined as "the connection that binds two bones or two joints together." If one isn't working properly, the whole body is affected. Sometimes rest can heal a damaged ligament, but other times major surgery is necessary.

Likewise, a wounded church member can weaken the entire body of Christ. We can help make sure our bodies are strong by taking good care of all its parts.

Today's Treasure

Caring for the ligaments in the body of Christ helps keep the whole church strong.

What can you do to help keep your church body healthy?

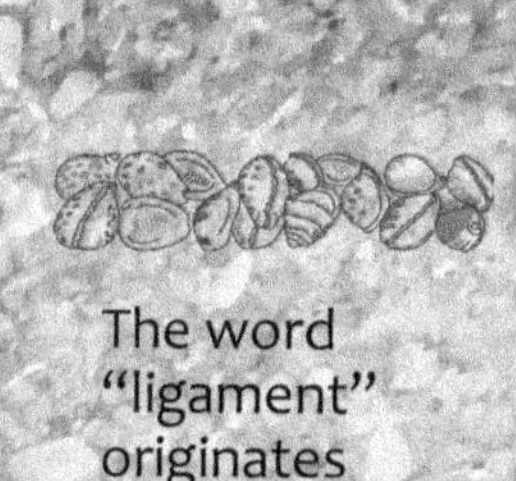

The word "ligament" originates from Latin for "to bind or bandage."

Money Cowrie
Cypraea moneta Linnaeus

Money cowries vary greatly in appearance. They are commonly used today in jewelry and decorations. At one time, they were also used as currency. You can find the one inch shells around coral reefs.

13

A Soothing Irritation

Iron sharpens iron, and one man sharpens another. ~ Proverbs 27:17

Cowries are mollusks similar to oysters. Both species have two valves inside held together by that all-important ligament. They also have an organ called a mantle that allows their shells to grow using minerals from the foods they eat. A substance called nacre lines the insides of both of them. Let's look at how God uses nacre to make pearls in the cowrie's cousin, the oyster.

When a foreign object, like sand, lodges between the mantle and the shell of an oyster, the tiny grain is so irritating that the oyster protects itself by releasing layer after layer of extra nacre. Over time, so much nacre is built up that a beautiful pearl is created out of the nuisance.

God can use the same method within us to create hearts devoted to Him.

When we live in community with others, issues are bound to creep in. My old Sunday school class wasn't called "Iron Sharpens Iron" for nothing. Often the people we are closest to are the ones who most easily get under our skin.

And yet, God uses family, *ohana*, to shape us into people who share His characteristics. Rubbing up against each other may be trying, but by allowing the nacre of His grace to flow over our rough edges, those irritations can transform us into an amazing array of pearls in angelic sizes and colors.

Oysters don't invite these irritations into their lives, any more than we do. But the resulting pearls are worth it.

Today's Treasure

Allow God's nacre of grace to flow over the sharp edges of your life to create a more exquisite pearl.

What rough spots in your character may need to be smoothed out with God's grace?

Beauty in the Breaking

I have refined you, but not as silver; I have tried you in the furnace of affliction. ~ Isaiah 48:10

The brilliant cowrie shell is polished to a lustrous gloss by an abrasive lime chemical it releases as lubrication to move across the ocean floor. The churning motion of the sea also enhances its shine. The sheen created by these irritations is one of the reasons cowries have been prized for centuries.

Can it be that our lives are sometimes buffed to a luminous glow by the agitations swirling around in our lives? Can the forces that shatter us be the same ones that strengthen us? Does God allow us to experience adversity for our benefit, as well as for the benefit of others? Could it be that pain can both harm and heal us?

Artists uncover a pretty purple color by applying muriatic acid to cowrie shells. After a burning period, the shells are rinsed in water to prevent too much deterioration. In this way, a deeper layer of the shell is revealed. This technique is used to carve intricate designs onto the tops of tiger cowries.

God uses the same method when He puts the details into the artwork of our lives. Getting rid of those crusted-on layers of corrosion exposes our weaknesses. No doubt, it can be painful. But, it also brings out an inner beauty that would otherwise be hidden.

Isaiah refers to this as the "refiner's fire." When the heat turns up, meltdowns can begin. Removing a crusty layer or two from the surface helps the good stuff inside rise to the top. That's why God takes off the gunk that hides the true beauty within us.

On one of my "ugly" days, I asked God why he didn't make me more beautiful on the outside. In His still small voice, He whispered, "Because I want people to look at you and see My beauty within."

God refines us in love to make us more like Him. However, our very real enemy, Satan, desires our destruction. He loves to see us battered, broken and beaten down by our trials. Satan's plan is to gouge us until we're "beach dull." God's plan is to love us and polish us up for His glory.

Unlike a shell, which when broken stays broken, God wants to heal our spirits and bring them to a new level of godliness. Impurities are burned away allowing our inner beauty to make us radiant. Then they are doused with oils of His mercy and grace. God's plan is always to make us more like Him. Satan's plan to scar us has already been redeemed by the scars of God's Son, Jesus. He took our burdens upon Himself when He died on the cross. Now He is resurrected in heaven, and we can reflect more of His Light to the world when His glow comes from within.

Today's Treasure

God uses everything that happens to us for good—even if the process sometimes hurts.

What rough areas in your life are being refined by God today?

The broken cowries I find remind me of some of the giants of the Christian faith who have been taken to places in life where their only hope was in the comfort of the cross. Either through the death of a loved one or living through other trying circumstances, their faith was tested to the point that they chose to give themselves over completely to God—no matter what the cost. They've come to trust that God loves them despite the circumstances that would make others walk away from their faith.

Focus on the Prize

*I press on toward the goal for the prize
of the upward call of God in Christ Jesus. ~ Philippians 3:14*

The Master Artist endlessly repaints the canvas of dawn, *wanaʻao*. Along the shoreline, skies are ever changing. The dance of the waves fluctuates between a graceful hula and a rousing rumba, and the sky swirls with color as the darkness slowly fades into *wanaʻao* and the *wanaʻao* welcomes daylight, *ao*.

Fresh tokens of the sea wrap the shoreline each morning. Souvenirs of sea glass, coral, and driftwood all call out for my attention. As I walk, I pause to look them over, but they are not what I'm here to find. My time is dedicated to searching for cowries as I listen to my heavenly Father's voice. So I keep my eyes and ears keenly focused on these goals. Otherwise, I won't complete the task that I am here for, the one He planned for me.

Cowries are a means of fulfilling God's commission to me as I walk and talk to Him. Avoiding the other tempting distractions around me, I set my sights on the sandy shores and rocky crevices. At times, I pull out my trusty spoon and dig in places where I think cowries may be uncovered. I pause often to listen and take notes on what I am hearing from God.

My focus needs to stay on my own commission. Other gifts lining the shore may be good things, but they aren't mine to pursue. They are there for others who have a different mission. The tasks given to me are different than those given to others, because we each have our own calling in Christ.

And yet, there is one goal that remains the same for all of us. Paul, the apostle and author of several letters in the Bible, reminds us to focus our lives on what really matters: to *know God and the power of His resurrection*...and share it with others. With that goal in mind, we won't lose our focus.

Today's Treasure

Keep your focus on treasures with eternal value, and you will find the ultimate prize.

How are you pursuing the path God has chosen for you?

Granulated Cowrie

Cypraea granuliata Pease, 1863
Leho ʻokala or leho opuʻopuʻ (rough or bumpy)

This rare cowrie is found in shallow water at depths of up to one hundred feet. It lives beneath rocks, in caves, and in deep cracks. An adult can reach up to one and a half inches in length.

Here I Am

*I will surely bless you, and I will surely multiply your offspring as the stars
of heaven and as the sand that is on the seashore. ~ Genesis 22:17*

Hawaiian beaches are covered in sands ranging in color from soft sparkling white to coarse volcanic black. There's even a Green Sand Beach on the southern point of the Big Island that was created by the breaking down of a volcanic semi-precious stone called olivine. No two pieces of the island's shoreline quilt are exactly alike. Each tiny grain is splendid with God's unique workmanship.

Early in the book of Genesis, God makes a promise to Abraham that he would have as many descendants on earth as there are sands on the shores.

Why did God give Abraham this promise?

God asked Abraham to climb Mount Moriah to offer Isaac as a sacrifice to Him. Abraham agreed to the task because of his faith in God, despite what would be immense personal loss. As he lifted his knife to complete the sacrifice, the Lord called out from heaven, "Abraham, Abraham."

"Here I am," Abraham replied.

At this moment of utter submission, a ram found in a nearby bush was substituted in Isaac's place, and an angel gave the promise to Abraham. These events foretell the substitution of God's own Son, Jesus, as a sacrifice for us. Centuries later, Jesus' willingness to shed His own blood in place of our own brings us forgiveness for our sins. Thankfully, it doesn't end there. Jesus rose up to heaven, giving us hope for our resurrection when our earthly lives are over.

And true to His word, both Jesus' spiritual descendants and Abraham's physical descendants fill the world today. Each one is as uniquely beautiful as the miniscule bits of sand that blanket Hawai'i's beaches.

Today's Treasure

God honors obedient hearts.

Are you willing to say to God, "Here I am"?

Isabella Cowrie

Cypraea Isabella Linnaeus

Lehokupeʻelema range in length from one half inch to two inches long. These common shells can be found from the tidal zone to depths of up to seventy feet. The largest ones are usually found in shallow water. Hawaiians have long used them for bracelets called *kupeʻe lima*.

21

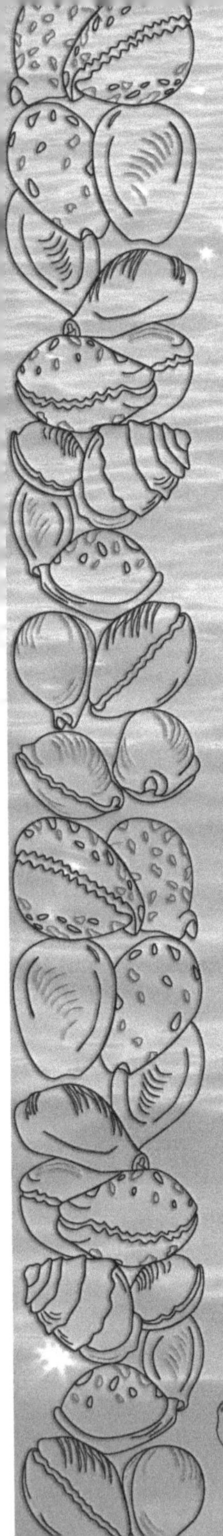

Love Written on Stone

We love because he first loved us. ~ 1 John 4:19

"Father, it's such a beautiful morning. You know how much I love the gifts You send me in these tide pools. Can you please send a special treasure today?"

I speak these words to my heavenly Father while strolling across the rugged volcanic shoreline in search of cowrie shells. As soon as the prayer leaves my mouth, I round a bend and instantly find His tender response.

The words "I love you" are carefully written out in large easy-to-read letters with pieces of the white coral that often wash up on this beach, *kahakai.* Locally called "Hawaiian graffiti," the pale block font contrasts sharply with its ebony lava backdrop, as if adding an exclamation point to His passionate words. The simplicity of the message speaks deeply to this beachcomber's heart.

I was praying for a cowrie treasure, but God the Creator had a better idea—a love note to me from my loving Papa.

"I love You, too, Abba."

Today's Treasure

God's gift of love is waiting for you.

Have you received the gift of His love into your heart?

I
LOVE
YOU

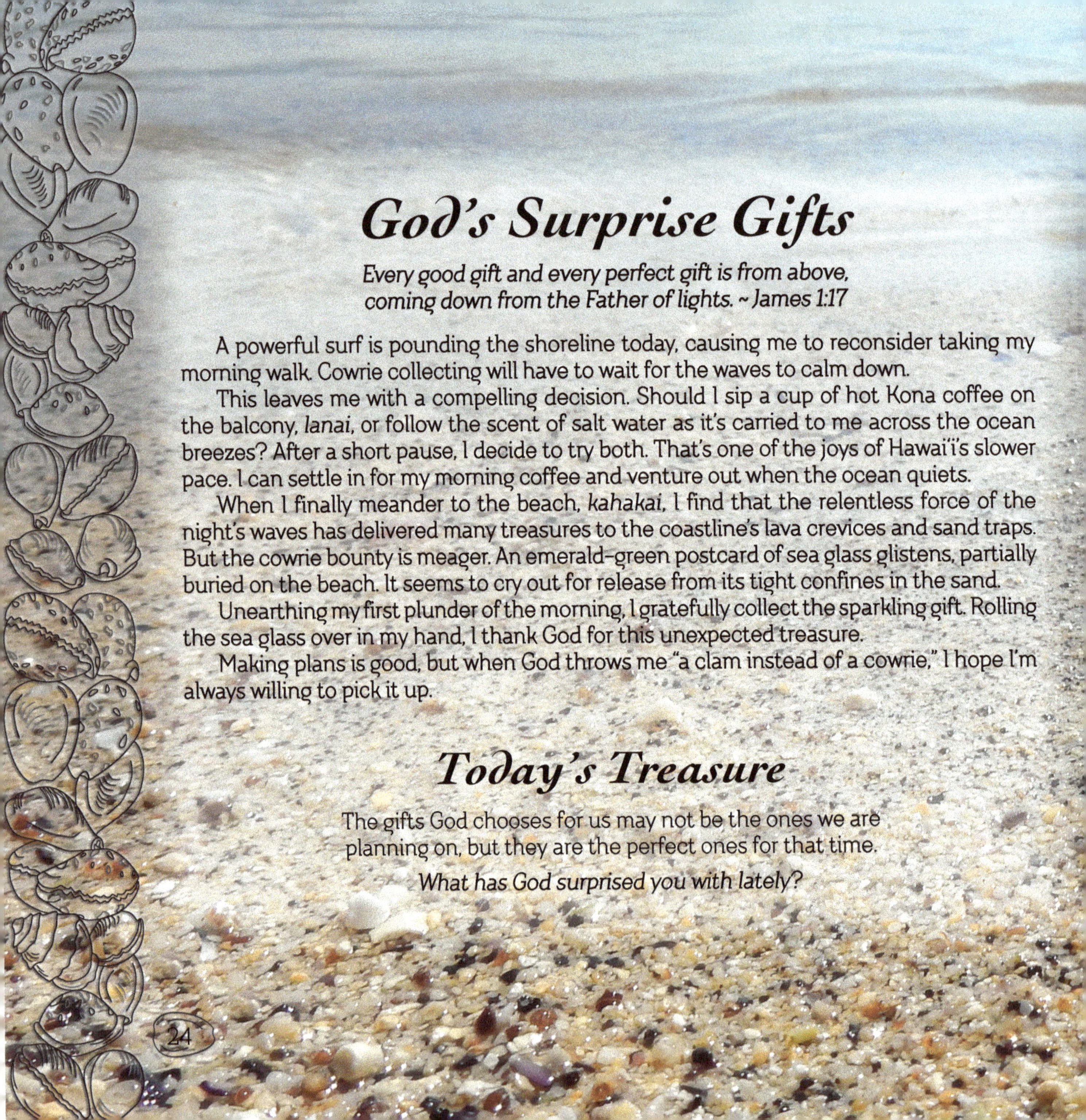

God's Surprise Gifts

Every good gift and every perfect gift is from above,
coming down from the Father of lights. ~ James 1:17

A powerful surf is pounding the shoreline today, causing me to reconsider taking my morning walk. Cowrie collecting will have to wait for the waves to calm down.

This leaves me with a compelling decision. Should I sip a cup of hot Kona coffee on the balcony, *lanai*, or follow the scent of salt water as it's carried to me across the ocean breezes? After a short pause, I decide to try both. That's one of the joys of Hawai'i's slower pace. I can settle in for my morning coffee and venture out when the ocean quiets.

When I finally meander to the beach, *kahakai*, I find that the relentless force of the night's waves has delivered many treasures to the coastline's lava crevices and sand traps. But the cowrie bounty is meager. An emerald-green postcard of sea glass glistens, partially buried on the beach. It seems to cry out for release from its tight confines in the sand.

Unearthing my first plunder of the morning, I gratefully collect the sparkling gift. Rolling the sea glass over in my hand, I thank God for this unexpected treasure.

Making plans is good, but when God throws me "a clam instead of a cowrie," I hope I'm always willing to pick it up.

Today's Treasure

The gifts God chooses for us may not be the ones we are planning on, but they are the perfect ones for that time.

What has God surprised you with lately?

Brett's Story

Although I have loved cowries since I was a child, their "specialness meter" shot way up after I went snorkeling with my teenage son a few years ago. Brett is a brilliant, funny, and compassionate young man, but we shared few common interests at the time.

I remember my excitement one perfect summer day, when Brett and I put on our snorkel gear and stepped into the warm tropical water together. After a few minutes of watching the undersea world unfold before us, Brett began pointing enthusiastically toward a colorful growth of coral.

"What do you see?" I slurred through my snorkel.

More emphatic gesturing on his part didn't help me understand. This frustrating non-communication went on for a few more minutes with no success.

Finally, exasperated, he dove down about ten feet. Resurfacing, he held up a four-inch-long, flawless tiger cowrie. The shell was a rich golden brown topped with leopard-like black spots.

It was the most perfect cowrie I'd ever seen. And I got to share this moment with my elusive son. On top of that, he seemed as excited as I was with the find! I wanted to cry for joy.

The shell is now prominently displayed in our home, along with the following poem, which I wrote about the double blessing. I don't think Brett knew about my special love for cowries at that time. Only the God who knows me so well could gift me in this personal way.

Today's Treasure

God knows every secret of your heart and shows you His love like a father to his child.

When have you been amazed by the personal way God showed His love to you?

27

Abba's Gift

Yesterday I went snorkeling with my son

To catch a glimpse of another world:

Corals

Fish

Lava

Blue.

Pointing!

Where?

A sudden dive to reveal

Abba's gift!

A cowrie.

Childhood memories only my Daddy would know.

A cowrie.

Sweet treasure He longs to bestow.

Tiger Cowrie

Cypraea tigris

No two tiger cowries are identical. They range in color from black or brown to white with large dark speckles. They can be found in gift shops throughout the Indo-Pacific with intricate designs carved into their shells. Hawaiian tiger cowries are active during the day, unlike most other cowries. They grow up to six inches in length and live in the open near reefs. This is the species of cowrie I found while snorkeling with my son Brett.

Uniquely Splendid

There is one glory of the sun, and another glory of the moon, and another glory of the stars; for star differs from star in glory. ~ 1 Corininthians 15:41

From the large tiger cowrie to the diminutive money cowrie, each species found in the world has its own perfect design. Their diverse shapes, sizes, and colors are individually fashioned by God to help them thrive in their natural environments.

At least thirty-three of the 250+ species of cowries in the world can be found in Hawai'i. That uniqueness suits every shell to its purpose. I wouldn't wear four-inch tiger cowries as a pendant— or especially as a pair of earrings. My *fashionista* scores would definitely be dinged for gaudiness. Besides, I'm not really fond of pierced-ear holes the size of nickels or in developing the posture of a famous humpback who once lived in Paris. Still, the tiger cowrie's shiny leopard-skin coat does make a wonderful focal point for display art, and its size makes it excellent for engraving.

On the other hand (or neck or ears), the one-inch-long money cowrie is just the right size and weight for jewelry, purses and other tropical trimmings. Shell leis are often crafted by stringing them together into a necklace. The money cowrie has been used as money (hence its name) in many cultures for centuries, partly because of its light weight. In fact, money cowrie was mentioned several times as a form currency in the African saga, *Roots*.

Just for fun, let's use these very different cowries in a little demonstration. Let's pretend the tiger cowrie decides it wants to be a form of currency because it would like to get out and travel more. (Okay, maybe cowries don't think. We're just pretending.) And the money cowrie dreams of taking center stage because it seems so glamorous. I don't need to tell you how silly this is.

But how often do we do this as people? It's so much easier to fit the job we are designed for, yet we often try to fit into someone else's flip flops, *slippahs*. Sometimes, positions that should be held by persons with the right giftings are filled by people with different giftings. This hurts the whole body.

Forcing our feet into the wrong pair of slippahs leads to frustration for everyone affected by the misfit. Especially for the people who spend a lifetime in discontent, when the simple remedy would be walking in their own unique purposes.

If you find yourself trying to squeeze a baby toe into a shoe that's too tight, then putting bandages on blisters, you may want to find a better fit. Wearing the slippahs precisely crafted to fit our own feet will always be more comfortable than trying to squeeze into someone else's slippahs.

Today's Treasure

Walk in the slippahs that are molded to fit your feet only.

Where is your comfortable fit?

Beautifully Broken

The sacrifices of God are a broken spirit; a broken and contrite heart,
O God, you will not despise. ~ Psalm 51:17

When does a broken piece of shell become a beautiful piece of art? When it is set in the right place.

Remember Jamie, the cowrie artist? She takes each tiny shard she finds and places it thoughtfully into the perfect position for the work she envisions. Each shell has a unique purpose. One highlights, a second shades, and another is used for accent. In the same way, we each have a place and purpose for our lives.

When our hearts are humbly broken before the Master Craftsman, His hand gently weaves us into our perfect places in the world's tapestry. The All-Seeing, All-Loving Father carefully designed a special place for each of us in His creation. The color of our skin, the shape of our bodies, the events of our lives, and the desires of our hearts were all purposely planned so we would fit snugly into our places. When our hearts are humbled, He makes beauty from ashes. You are different from the people around you, but your presence influences each of them in some way. They affect others around them. And when we are all woven together, our lives impact the world.

Today's Treasure

Submit your heart to God and He will put you in your perfect place.

Will you take some time to humbly offer yourself to God,
so He can place you in the masterpiece He is creating?

Gathering Together

*Let us consider how to stir up one another to love and good works,
not neglecting to meet together. ~ Hebrews 10:24–25*

On March 11, 2011, an earthquake on the far side of the Pacific thrust the sea onto the shores of Hawai'i. Damage here wasn't nearly as devastating as in Japan, but the tidal wave, *tsunami*, unearthed some unusual shells from the ocean floor.

Some of the shells I found shortly after the wave were tiny, snail-like cones similar to the prized Ni'ihau shells. I wasn't the only one surprised to find them on the Big Island. A young mother and her son were gathering them alongside me.

"Why do you suppose so many of these shells are pooled together in this place?" she asked me.

The only thought that came to my mind was *birds of a feather flock together*.

The sea life that once inhabited these shells lived in community on the seabed. They remained together in their journey to the shore, even as they were upheaved by the monster sea.

Nature seems to reinforce God's plan for sharing life together. The church is the gathering place for Christians. This is where we share life (and death). Romans 12:1 tells us to rejoice with those who rejoice; mourn with those who mourn. When we rejoice together, eat together, worship together, go through blessings and crises together, we are living in the unity of God's Spirit.

After a powerful wave of the Holy Spirit fell on the apostles in the second chapter of Acts, the Bible says, all those who believed were together and had all things in common.

This is one of the blessings I love most about being part of the family, *ohana*, of God. Our human nature thrives in community, just as it does for all of creation.

Today's Treasure

God planned for us to share life in community with other believers.

Who are the people you consider ohana?

Families work together creating beautiful shell jewelry on the northern Hawaiian island of Niʻihau. Captain Cook, who charted the "Sandwich Isles" (Hawaiʻi) owned a Niʻihau shell lei. Money cowries form the petals of this bracelet.

When Seasons Change

For everything there is a season, and a time for every matter under heaven.
~ Ecclesiastes 3:1

The 2001 tsunami that hit Hawai'i changed the shoreline's landscape. Lava tide pools were transformed into sandy beaches. Brackish waters flowed into the ocean and are now one with it. New shells and old ones spread into different habitats in the offshore waters. Some were unearthed from the ocean floor and brought to the beaches after slumbering for years.

At first, I didn't see many fully intact cowries in their usual spots, but I did come upon large pieces of broken cowries. Perhaps the flood sent currents from new directions, or the tide was carrying the sea's treasures to divergent fingers of the land.

These changes baffled me a bit in the beginning. But they weren't confusing to God. His control over all of nature is demonstrated repeatedly in the Bible, from the appearance of a rainbow to the rumble of an earthquake.

And so it is, one season, *kau*, ends and a new one begins. The change may be temporary, or it may last a lifetime. Each season offers its own set of opportunities and challenges. I often pause to realign my compass in the direction the Father is guiding. Sometimes He directs me along one path, and then He veers off in another direction. As time goes on, I'm learning to adjust my expectations to these obvious changes.

It seems life is a series of switchbacks. As long as I keep checking in with Him for guidance, I trust I will find my way.

Today's Treasure

Each new set of waves must be ridden with God's hand on the rudder.

What season do you find yourself in at this time?

37

A Familiar Voice

So he was there with the Lord forty days and forty nights. He neither ate bread nor drank water. And he wrote on the tablets the words of the covenant, the Ten Commandments. ~ Exodus 34:28

The Hawaiian conch shell, *pu,* can be heard up to two miles away. It is used as a means of fanfare, to signal the beginning of a ceremony, or to accompany chants. Its volume is adjusted by how the shell is blown, not by how much air is blown into it.

After an extended trip off the island, I returned to the beach, looking for cowries. But the once familiar shoreline felt a little foreign to me. Partly due to my absence and partly because of changes the tsunami created, it took some time to reacquaint myself with my surroundings.

Even my normally easy communication with God seemed somewhat out of sync. I knew He was listening, but for some reason my hearing was a little scratchy.

Moses spent numerous days alone with God, so when God spoke to him, he knew it. There was no question about who was speaking to him. The time Moses spent with God made His voice easy to hear and clear to understand. As a result, Moses was able to receive the Ten Commandments and then communicate God's instructions to the Israelites for forty years in the desert.

As I meandered along the beach that first day back, I uncovered many broken bits of cowrie before finding any shells that were fully intact. In much the same way, the little bytes of sound I heard from God at first eventually grew into clear conversation. By the end of my walk, I felt as if I were meeting up with an old friend after a long separation. Our talk flourished into heart-to-heart communication.

If you are not used to hearing God speak to you, you may want to set aside some quiet time to listen. His voice becomes clearer with time and practice.

Today's Treasure

The more you converse with God, the easier it is to recognize His voice.

Are you able to sense the voice of God as He speaks to your spirit?

Sing to God a brand new song,
sing His praises all over the world!
Let the sea and its fish give
a round of applause,
with all the far-flung islands joining in.

Isaiah 42:10

Get in the Water

*Again he sent other servants, saying, "Tell those who are invited,
'See, I have prepared my dinner, my oxen and my fat calves have been slaughtered,
and everything is ready. Come to the wedding feast.'" ~ Matthew 22:4*

When my mother came to Hawai'i, we spent hours drinking coffee together on the balcony, *lanai*. As the mornings lingered on, our leisurely conversations continued at one of Hawai'i's many relaxing beaches. Later, as I snorkeled out to a coral reef in search of colorful fish or cowries, Mom chose to stay cool beneath her shady coconut tree. (Perhaps that's why she looked twenty years younger than her actual age.) Evenings were often spent at one of our favorite beachfront restaurants, listening to Hawaiian music while waves lazily lapped on the shore.

Toward the end of one of her vacations, I realized Mom hadn't touched the sea, *moana*, at all. She'd sat in her beach chair for hours, admiring the view, but never ventured past the dry sand. So on the day of her departure, I decided to change that!

Stopping at the beach in front of my home, I told her she couldn't get on the plane without at least dabbling her toes in the seawater. Her reaction of surprise and excitement told me this thought had never occurred to her! She started toward the shoreline, leaving her footprints in the wet sand. I watched happily as she rolled up the cuffs on her black polyester pants and tentatively touched the edge of a wave sliding onto the shore.

It didn't take long for her to realize what she'd been missing all those years. I grabbed my camera and snapped photos of her looking like a young child, *keiki*, playing in the surf for the first time. She was truly having fun!

This wonderful memory we shared only happened because I invited her to get into the water. She was a willing participant, but she needed the invitation to step into the ocean.

Do you know someone who might want to join you in the living waters of life with Christ? Perhaps that person just needs a nudge in the right direction. Maybe, like my mother, he or she has been watching from afar and is just waiting for an invitation to get in.

Today's Treasure

Throwing out an invitation may become someone's Lifesaver.

Who can you invite to get into the Living Waters with you?

On the second anniversary of my mother's death, I returned to the beach where Mom had timidly touched the ocean. Another woman was gingerly approaching the water while her husband cheered her on. Within moments, she was giggling, splashing, playing, and posing while her husband snapped photos of her. The memory of my mother doing the same made me smile.

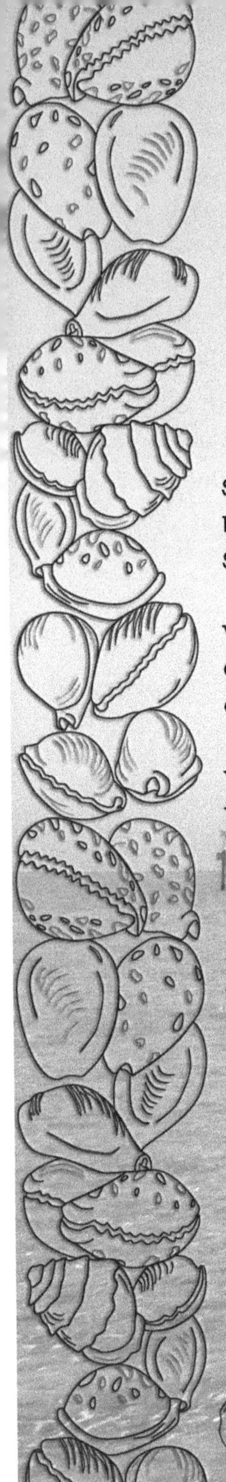

Come on In

Even before I asked Mom to touch the warm Hawaiian waters, she admired the aquamarine shoreline. She'd spend hours observing from her comfortable beach chair, cheering me on in my quest to find shells. Like an avid sports fan watching her favorite team from the sidelines, she applauded the game but didn't play it. I'm glad she finally accepted my invitation to get in.

I'm sure Mom felt a bit awkward approaching the water. After all, she'd spent eighty-five years on the sidelines. But it didn't take long for her to realize what she'd been missing out on. I wonder what she could have done if she'd started swimming earlier in life. She may have dived in deeper and deeper as she began to realize all the treasures of the undersea world.

God offers all of us a standing invitation to enter into His living waters. He calls His waters living because they bring eternal life. Jesus never says no when you ask Him to be your Lifesaver. Accepting the gift of God's Son into your heart is all it takes to become one of His children. And you'll immediately find yourself showered with every good and perfect gift (James 1:) that is part of your inheritance from Him as His child.

As a bonus, He offers free swim lessons while you get used to the water! All you need to know can be found in His survival manual, the Bible. And other believers will come alongside you to help with your training. You may start out dog-paddling, but with practice you will learn the Master's strokes. Let yourself become fully immersed in the waters that will quench your thirst forever. Come on in—the water's fine!

Today's Treasure

Dive into the Water of Life that satisfies like no other.

Have you accepted God's invitation to enter into the waters of eternal life with Him?

Humpback Cowrie (Lehoahi)

Cypraea mauritiana Linnaeius

This brownish-black cowrie is mottled with irregular light markings. The rather pointed curve of its back lends it to being used for grating coconuts and preparing kappa (bark cloth). Shells with a dark reddish color and smaller spots are called ipo (sweetheart) and were used as octopus lures in ole Hawai'i. The cowrie lives in the intertidal zone and can be up to five and a half inches long.

Facing Loss

Weeping may tarry for the night, but joy comes with the morning. ~ Psalm 30:5

The forceful pull of the moon, in its unceasing journey to light up our night skies, influences the ebbs and flows of our ocean tides. When the waters retreat, they take some treasures out with them, but other trinkets are left behind on the beach for collecting. The surf gives and the surf takes away.

I walked the beach on my mother's birthday the year after she went to heaven. Four plumerias washed ashore in the waves at the same place Mom got in the water. How she loved those flowers! I thanked God for giving me these four little tokens to assure me that my mom was well and sending her love to each one in the family. (One flower for each of her three children and one for my husband.) On the next anniversary of her birthday, I found a unique shell resting out in the open like a gift on the shore.

When I lost my mother, I didn't want to let her go, even though I knew it was her time. God didn't plan death, destruction, loss, or pain. They came into the world as the result of disobedience (sin) in the Garden of Eden. Yet He provides hope and redemption through the sacrificial death and resurrection of His Son, Jesus, on the cross. After He died, Jesus rose again, and now He lives eternally with His Father in heaven. Through the cross, God redeems the losses we face in this life. And we hold on to the hope of life eternal with our loved ones in heaven, *lani.*

Today's Treasure

God knows our sorrows and gives us a promise of peace and hope in heaven.

What losses can you give to God to carry you through a painful season?

On April Fool's Day 1946, a series of three tidal waves came ashore at Lapauhoehoe on the Big Island. The first two waves pulled the ocean out, exposing the seabed. Twenty-three students and four teachers ran out to collect the ocean treasures lying before them. The third wave was larger than the first two and overtook all of them. This catastrophic event is recognized as one of the biggest tragedies ever to hit Hawai'i. But the grief that followed led to a better tsunami warning system throughout the islands.

When my friend Jennie visited, we saw a beautiful rainbow over Lapauhoehoe cutting through a stormy gray sky. The next year, Jennie unexpectedly went to be with the Lord. As I prayed for comfort that day, I asked God to send me a sign that Jennie was in His presence in heaven. He doesn't always answer this in such a clear way, but that day He did. A gorgeous rainbow appeared over my home church. I'd never seen one there before.

Just like the rainbow after a storm, God has sent His light into the world to overcome the darkness, bringing with it hope and peace for each new day.

Digging for Gold

If you receive my words and treasure up my commandments…if you call out for insight and raise your voice for understanding, if you seek it like silver and search for it as for hidden treasures, then you will understand the fear of the Lord and find the knowledge of God. ~ Proverbs 2:1–5

A remote tropical island. A swashbuckling sword fight. A faded map with clues leading to buried treasure, where X marks the spot. And just offshore, a fair maiden walks the plank, hoping to be saved before plunging into the ocean depths. Such is the stuff pirate movies are made of when in search of hidden riches.

While I don't have a big X to mark the spot or a treasure map leading the way, my search for cowries leads me on a quest to find my own bounty. The shells often lie in patches of potpourri on the shore, but they can be buried inside coastal crevices. I shovel, dig, pull, and pick them from their diverse resting places.

We all have hidden treasure buried in our hearts. Good gifts—like love, hope, joy, peace, and compassion—are ours when we accept them from our heavenly Father.

But sometimes these gifts are buried in unwanted slime. When jealously, fear, or unforgiveness have lodged themselves in the depths of our hearts, the roots can grip our innermost beings, strangling the good fruits. We may be so accustomed to their presence that we are unaware of their effects. Or perhaps we realize we have garbage buried within but don't know how to dig it out. These hidden sins must be uprooted.

Allowing God to delve into your dark places will set your spirit free. The key to releasing God's riches is allowing the Word of God to replace any lies you have believed with the treasure trove of God's truth. Studying the Bible and praying with strong believers are great tools to accomplish this.

Our spiritual gifts dwell within us, waiting to be acknowledged, revealed, and incorporated into our lives. God wants you to claim your stake and be set free from the world's entrapments that have held your heart prisoner.

His love is gold, which never rusts. And the silver you'll find is God's wisdom and understanding. Your life will glitter as the gifts of the Spirit shine through you.

The treasures of heaven are the only ones worth walking the plank for.

Today's Treasure

If you walk the plank of faith, be assured that God will catch you on the other end.

Where does your treasure lie?

Fertile Ground

As for that in the good soil, they are those who, hearing the word, hold it fast in an honest and good heart, and bear fruit with patience. ~ Luke 8:15

After some experience at beachcombing, I've come to recognize places on the beach that look like they may yield some cowries. The sand may still be damp and untouched sea rubble lies scattered along the shore. The high tide line is bordered with cowries and other gifts the waves have left behind. This area is ripe for harvest.

Jesus told His disciples about how to recognize "good sand." This parable, as recorded in Luke 8:1-15, is about a farmer who sows his seeds in four types of soil: hard, rocky, thorny, and soft. Jesus explains that these four soils represent four types of human hearts. Each one is given the opportunity to hear the word of God, but each responds to it differently.

People with hard hearts don't take the time to listen when they are told the good news. Since the seed doesn't take root, it immediately dies.

Those with rocky hearts hear the truth but don't apply it to their lives. Their roots are not watered or fertilized, and soon they wither up without bearing fruit.

When the seed of God's word is sown in thorny hearts, the hearers try to obey the Bible, but they give up when trials or distractions test them. Weeds choke out the fruit and steal the nutrients needed for growth. They are uprooted with the weeds growing alongside them.

Thankfully, some hearts are full of soil that is soft and fertile for receiving the word of God. They readily accept the seed when it is planted, water it wisely, and cultivate it with time to send down deep roots. The seeds grow and the fruit flourishes in their lives. These hearts find nurture and love in God's care.

God leads me to fertile sand to find cowries. Let's prepare good soil in our hearts, so we can reap a bountiful harvest for His kingdom.

Today's Treasure

God is looking for hearts with fertile soil ready to produce good fruit.

What kind of soil do you think can be found in your heart?

At the Puako Petropglyph Archaeological Preserve on the Big Island, more than 1,200 ancient petroglyphs are viewable to the public. In Hawaiian, they are called *k'i'i pohaku* (images in stone). Dating back hundreds of years, they are thought to record births, deaths and other important events in the lives of early Hawaiians.

Depositing the Goods

*Lay up for yourselves treasures in heaven, where neither moth
nor rust destroys and where thieves do not break in and steal.
For where your treasure is, there your heart will be also. ~ Matthew 6:20–21*

It's not possible to take home everything I find on my walks, so I only keep some of the cowries and other trinkets I discover. The ones I deem most valuable come home with me.

Each of us makes choices about what we think is important. Every day, we are bombarded with messages, many of which are conflicting. When we learn something new about God's character, we decide whether to hold on to it or throw it away. When we choose to make it part of our own character, we are storing up riches that will stay with us forever. That is something we can't collect too much of.

As much as I love gathering cowries, I know they won't go with me when I leave this world. But when God shows me a new truth from His Word, the choice I make to plant it in my heart holds eternal value. Each new gem I store is added to the treasure chest that already lives within me. As my heart radiates new facets of His glory, my hope is that this wealth will flow to the people I meet. These are riches that cannot be stolen.

Today's Treasure

When we store God's Word in the fertile soil of our hearts,
it is best used by transplanting it into the lives of others.

What aspect of God's truth would you like to add to the garden of your heart today?

Reticulated Cowrie

Cypraea maculifera Schilder

In Hawai'i, this cowrie is also called *leho kolea* (like a net) named after the Pacific Golden Plover, *kolea*, a migratory bird with similar markings. It can reach two and a half inches in length and lives in cracks and shaded areas from the shoreline to around fifty feet deep.

The Armor of God

Therefore take up the whole armor of God, that you may be able to withstand in the evil day, and having done all, to stand firm. ~ Ephesians 6:13

The cowrie shell is actually an external skeleton that protects the mollusk's soft body within. Newborn cowries don't have shells when they are born, so the tiny transparent creatures make easy prey. Thankfully for them, after just a few days, mineral crystals build up to create a shell around the snail. Soon the layers are thick enough to provide protection, so the cowrie can come out when it is safe or pull inside for shelter. The resplendent markings on their shells are often designed to camouflage the mollusks from their predators.

When we are born again, it takes us some time to learn how to live the Christian life within God's shelter. The moment we ask Jesus to be our Savior and Lord, we inherit all the blessings of being one of God's children. However, we, too, have predators who would seek to devour us if we are not wise. Our battles are against the forces of Satan, who would love to maintain control over our lives. Temptations to sin can lure us into doing things we know we shouldn't, especially if they're habits we've had for a long time. Knowing when it's safe to venture out and when we need to retreat is an important lesson for us to learn.

God lays out the wardrobe for our daily spiritual protection in Ephesians 6. It's called the "armor of God," and it can be worn beneath even the most fashionable attire.

First, He tells us to buckle the *belt of truth* around our waists. The Word of God is worn at a central place on our bodies. If we wrap our lives around the things God tells us are true, they will be accessible when we need to pull them out and use when we are making decisions or need discernment.

Next, we are told to place the *breastplate of righteousness* over our hearts and fit our feet with the *gospel of peace*. For defense, we carry the *shield of faith* and place the *helmet of salvation* on our heads. Finally, taking up the *sword of the Spirit* , listening to God wherever we go, we cover ourselves with *prayer*. To stay spiritually healthy, beginning each day with prayer is like taking our daily multivitamin.

Getting dressed for the day without preparing ourselves properly is like that baby cowrie swimming in the immense ocean unprotected. God is our shield and our strength.

I thank God for the protective clothing He offers us. I'm also grateful for His angels who do battle for us in the heavenly realm. God is already the victor in our spiritual battles when we take our stand with His perfect protection.

Today's Treasure

Be strong in the Lord and in His mighty power.

Are you wearing your protective armor as you venture into the world today?

A Cowrie's Armor

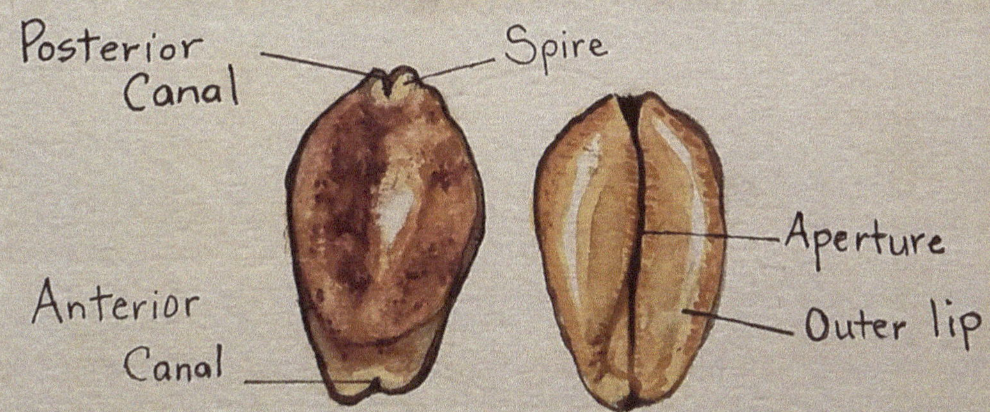

The mineral crystals that make up a cowrie's shell build up one layer at a time until the shell becomes hard. If this process happens slowly and continually, the shell becomes smooth. Rings or ridgelines will develop on the shell if there are pauses between growth spurts. Like trees, the more rings on a cowrie, the older the shell.

On the cowrie's bottom side, there is a narrow-toothed slit called an aperture. Only a few predators are able to gain access to the animal living within the shell because of this natural protection.

Cowrie shells are not only beautiful, they are well-designed. Similarly, when we wear God's spiritual attire, we are "dressed to kill" the attacks of any evil forces.

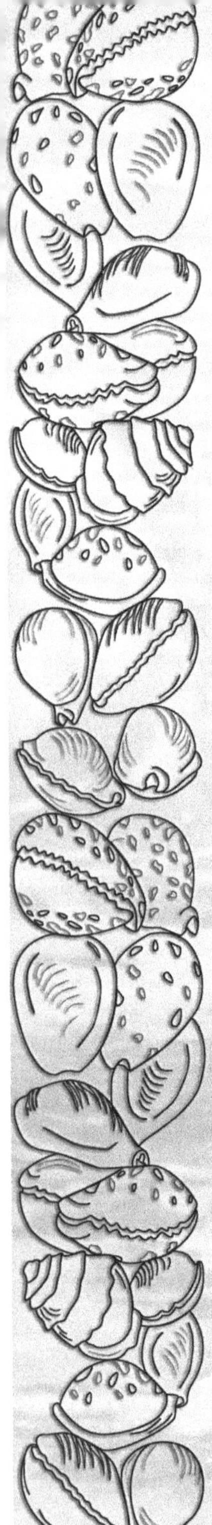

Seen from Within

For You formed my inward parts; You knitted me together in my mother's womb.
~ Psalm 139:13

Although I find only empty cowrie shells on the beach, a vulnerable snail once lived within this secure protection. The tender creature would surely be eaten alive by its predators if not for this hard, camouflaging coat of armor.

The tender human heart is also shielded by a physical body that hides it from predators. Not only does it insulate our organs, it guards our very soul. Beneath these external veneers, we all yearn for the same things: love, security, acceptance, joy, and freedom. God knows all about the person within. He is the one who knit us together before we were born.

In the garden of Eden, God designed man not only to survive but to thrive. Adam and Eve were living in paradise and felt no shame until they disobeyed Him. Then they tried to hide from their Creator behind a fig leaf. God desires truth and intimacy as we stand naked before Him. We are His bride and nothing can come between us and the love He has for us. God sees past our facades and into our hearts. His love goes beyond our flaws and failures.

Like the tender cowrie, we are tender and vulnerable within. But when we put our trust in our loving bridegroom, we are safe beneath the shelter of His love.

Today's Treasure

God is a strong shield about us, the lover of our souls.

Are you living in the shelter of God, your Creator and the Lover of your soul?

What's inside a cowrie shell?

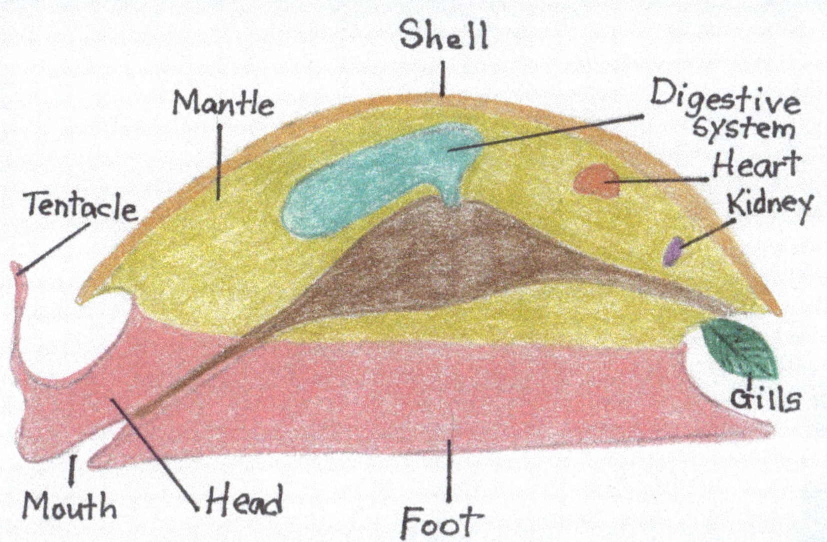

The Treasure of Being Known

O Lord, You have searched me and known me! ~ Psalm 139:1

An excited young surfer just ran past me on his way to joining his friends in the water. His look of anticipation tells me he's looking forward to a good ride. The surf must be high today. It's obvious he's just as passionate about his sport as I am about collecting cowries at the shore.

We both come to the same beach to find our treasures, though the treasures we seek are not the same. Looking for a great ride on the perfect wave, he runs right over the cowries I am here to find. His gaze is fixed on the sea.

God is able to satisfy the desires of both of our hearts. The waves that carry cowries to the shore bring joy to this surfer when he rides their curls. When the God Who Sees, *El Roi*, made us, He knew what would inspire us. He knew our passions. He created them.

God knows all about you and how to make you feel special. Whether it is a wave, a shell, or something else, Abba has a way of letting us know that He longs for a relationship that is uniquely personal with each of us.

Today's Treasure

God knows how to love you best.

How has God shown His love to you in a personal way?

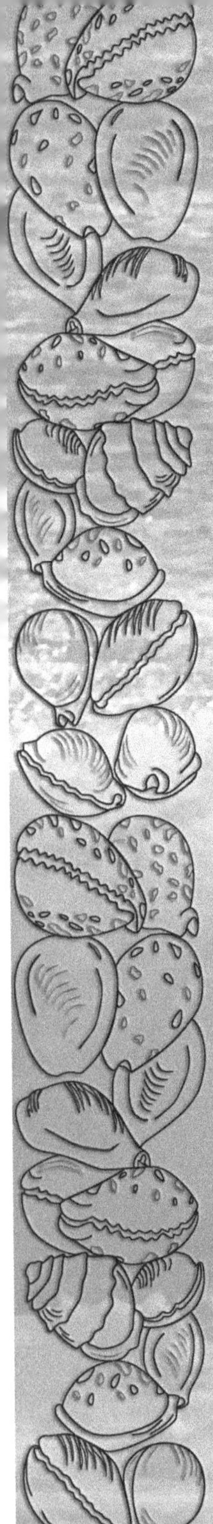

Catch the Wave

And the men marveled, saying, "What sort of man is this,
that even winds and sea obey him?" ~ Matthew 8:27

Can you imagine the disciples' shock when Jesus calmly told the waves and the wind on the Sea of Galilee to stop...and they did?

God still controls each wave as it rolls across the globe. In my search for cowries, I'm always keenly aware of what the waves are doing as they gently roll in or crash upon the shore. Knowing the ocean conditions is important for safety, as well as for judging when and where I am likely to find shells.

Keeping our eyes fixed on the wave of the Holy Spirit as He moves across the earth is always compelling. Catching His wave means flowing in sync with whatever He is doing at the moment. He's constantly changing things up. Sometimes He sends huge waves, spraying showers of blessings high into the sky. On those immense joy rides, you may hear me hooting and hollering praise to God. I liken it to surfers screaming, "Cowabunga!" as they conquer the pipeline. Other days I let sets of waves roll by while I peacefully bask in God in a turquoise lagoon of His peace.

I want to keep my eyes open and my heart prepared to go anywhere with the Spirit. I trust that the tides He controls will always take me in the right direction. Unlike most surfers, who prefer less crowded waves, I hope that you will join me as we hang ten riding the tide of God's wave that flows with the wind.

Today's Treasure

You'll have the ride of your life when you catch the wave of the Holy Spirit!

Are you on board with what the Holy Spirit is doing in your life?

If it's been a while since you've watched for the wave of the Holy Spirit in your life, you may want to ease into the water… just as surfers start out on small waves and move up to the bigger ones with practice. Large waves are easy to see, and you can join in whenever you're ready.

Unfathomable God

Have you not known? Have you not heard? The Lord is the everlasting God, the Creator of the ends of the earth. He does not faint or grow weary; his understanding is unsearchable. ~ Isaiah 40:28

I love the word *unfathomable*. It stirs up the deep and mysterious recesses of my mind. The Bible reminds me that I, as one of God's created beings, can't even begin to understand the essence of who our unfathomable God is.

Looking out over the vast sea, my imagination takes me to that eerie world where bioluminescent oddities drift in pitch-black ocean depths, many carrying their own sources of light. This expansive abyss exists not in "a galaxy far, far away," but in a large hidden portion of our own watery planet.

This strange undersea world reflects a dimension of God's creation rarely seen by mankind. And yet God knows each of these organisms' comings and goings, just as He does ours. That stretches the limits of my mind.

For centuries, philosophers have tried to unravel God's soul. But God is beyond human understanding. Faith is believing that God is who He says He is: YHWH, the Great I AM, the Creator of everything. The mysteries of life and time lie within this unfathomable kingdom of God.

Today's Treasure

We will never fathom the depths of who God is.

What questions within your heart may never be answered until you meet Him in heaven?

We are deep
But God is
deeper.
We are His
But He is.
Can you
fathom this?

One fathom is six feet (two yards) deep. In Hawai'i, cowries live in depths of up to thirty-four fathoms.

Do you not know?
Have you not heard?
The Lord is the everlasting God,
the Creator of the ends of the earth.
He will not grow tired or weary,
and His understanding no one can fathom.
Isaiah 40:28 NIV

Fire and Water

*And we know that for those who love God all things work together for good,
for those who are called according to his purpose. ~ Romans 8:28*

In my ongoing search for cowries along Hawai'i's changeable shoreline, I sometimes hike across rough lava. At other times my feet sink sweetly into soft sand. Volcanic explosions that send the red-hot lava into the ocean are still forming these islands through a constant brew of fire and water.

We all tread unpredictable paths in life, through a sizzling blend of trials and treasures that make us who we are. When the 'a'a explodes around us, our paths get rocky. The smoother lava, *paho'eho'e*, surrounds more rhythmic and smoother times.

I savor the good times, when I am blessed with joy in my life. But even in the darkest times, I trust that God is at work, preparing me for eternity with Him. He uses the perfect blend of fire and water to simmer His character into my life.

Today's Treasure

Both fire and water are necessary for the refining transformation of our hearts.

In the timeline of your life, what experiences has God used to shape your being?

The lava fields across these islands are permanent reminders of the opposing forces that brought this paradise into existence. The 2018 eruption of Kilauea volcano added about 875 acres of new land to the Big Island. The sky was filled with huge plumes of steam, made up of glass particles and corrosive acid mist, where the land and sea met to create this new terrain.

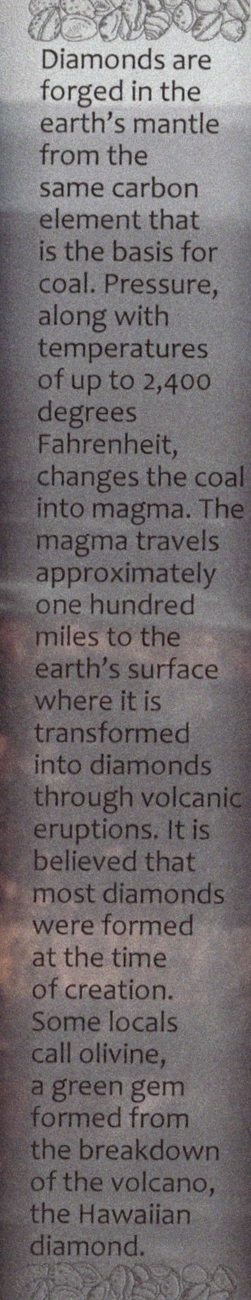

Diamonds are forged in the earth's mantle from the same carbon element that is the basis for coal. Pressure, along with temperatures of up to 2,400 degrees Fahrenheit, changes the coal into magma. The magma travels approximately one hundred miles to the earth's surface where it is transformed into diamonds through volcanic eruptions. It is believed that most diamonds were formed at the time of creation. Some locals call olivine, a green gem formed from the breakdown of the volcano, the Hawaiian diamond.

All Creation Sings

Let the sea roar, and all that fills it; the world and those who dwell in it!
~ Psalm 98:7

God designed more than 250 species of cowries to fill the earth's oceans. And that is just the beginning of His creativity in just one of the hundreds of species of shells. He derives pleasure from all that He makes. And cowries, in all their shapes and sizes, were created to glorify Him. Their beauty and diversity bring Him joy.

We were all created to worship God. The Bread of Life nourishes us spiritually as we honor Him, just as food and water nourish our physical bodies.

In Luke 19:40, the Bible tells us that if we don't choose to worship God, even the stones will cry out to Him. From the tiniest snail to the largest whale, every creature in the ocean, on the land, and in the sky was created to glorify the Creator God.

"I tell you...if they keep quiet, the stones will cry out" (Luke 19:40).

Today's Treasure

You are part of God's creation and made to worship Him.

How do you express your worship to God?

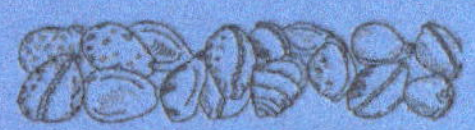

Spinner dolphins can be seen living in family groups along the coast of Hawaii. They are usually between four and eight feet long and weigh between 50 and 170 pounds. It's not unusual to see them as they jump and spin through the air. At night, they feed on small fish, squid and shrimp.

*Praise the Lord from the earth,
you great sea creatures
and all the ocean depths...Psalm 148:7*

The Hawaiian monk seal, *Ilio holo I ka uaua* (dog that runs in rough water), is the state mammal of Hawai'i. Adult males can reach seven feet in length and weigh between 300 and 400 pounds. Females are much larger reaching eight feet in length and weighing in at between 400 and 600 pounds. Most pups are born on beaches between March and June. Mom will not eat for 5-6 weeks while she protects her newborn, but she will abandon him and gain her weight back when she has weened her pup. The monk seal is currently considered an endangered species, so keep your distance if you see one.

Picking up the Broken Pieces

"For I know the plans I have for you, declares the Lord, plans for welfare
and not for evil, to give you a future and a hope." ~ Jeremiah 29:11

My first find today is quite thought provoking—half of a large tiger cowrie. Turning the broken piece over in my hand, I consider the beauty this shell once held—complete in the artistry of its Maker.

What force was so strong that it was able to break the strong mold specially designed to protect the fragile body held within? Did a predator force the life out of it, devouring its tender insides? Or was it the constant churning of the waves, continually pounding the shell upon the ocean floor? How long and how hard did the beating go on?

At some point, this cowrie couldn't take the assault anymore and broke in half. The splintered shell drifted to this beach, crippled and alone...its perfectly designed armor ripped apart...until it was hardly recognizable as the beautiful shell it once was.

Have you ever felt beaten down? Disconnected from those around you? Were the dreams you once held dear overtaken by fear and disappointment? Has your true identity in Christ been shattered by the scars of life? Perhaps even now you feel battered by the storms surrounding you. Once strong and vibrant, you now seem tossed aside and left alone to dry up in isolation.

God has a better plan. He wants you to live your life as His prized creation, in fullness and health. Give your hurts and sorrows to Him and let Him bring life back to you from the inside out. Ask Him to restore your hope for the future. He is able to bring the splintered pieces of your life back together and replace them with the beautiful garments of praise He fashioned just for you.

Today's Treasure

God plans for you to live a full and fruitful life.

What parts of your life do you need God to put back together for you?

Timing is Everything

*He has made everything beautiful in its time. He has also set eternity in the human heart;
yet no one can fathom what God has done from beginning to end. ~ Ecclesiastes 3:11 NIV*

Time slips away when I'm beachcombing. Before I know it, the sun, *la*, is peeking over the eastward mountain and the once quiet roads are filled with excited vacationers eager to embark on their Hawaiian adventures. All too soon, it's time to leave the beach to begin my daily duties.

While I may not be aware of the passing time, God's hand is firmly set on earth's pendulum. He coordinates everything from the moon and its tides to the heavenly backdrop of the sky and the stars. The sun is the catalyst for setting time zones around the world.

God sends each shell to this shore in its proper season, just as He synchronizes the day-to-day events of our lives. Nothing takes Him by surprise. He is the Great Architect, and He laid out the master blueprints before the world began.

When it seems that life's events are spinning out of control, it is comforting to know that God is at the helm, lining them up with military precision. When our own resources are depleted, the only One who can orchestrate harmony from chaos responds with His all-knowing, perfectly timed, "only God could have done that" answer. Our own insufficiencies make us realize how much we depend on Him, and that's a good thing to know as we go through this unpredictable life. Lately, I've even been contemplating the fact that God will actually move the universe in answer to our prayers.

God is preparing us to spend eternity with Him. He watches over every detail of our lives, with pin-point focus on our final destination. He sees the beginning and the end, and His promise is to make everything beautiful in its time. His pendulum is immeasurably more accurate than ours. It is set to the tempo of time eternal.

Today's Treasure

God is never early or late.

What seems out of control in your life that you are willing to place on God's time schedule?

Cowries are used for decoration on many specialty items. To keep cowries their shiniest, they should be kept out of direct sunlight and not cleaned with acids. Even on the shore in natural sunlight, their shells dull over time.

69

Seek to Find

If you seek Him, He will be found by you. ~ 1 Chronicles 28:9

Each wave sending its gifts to the shoreline is like the postman delivering Christmas presents to our doorsteps. What surprises does the wave hold within its watery wrappings? What trinkets will be left when the water retreats?

Like waves continually depositing their baubles onto the shoreline, the different infinite facets of God are constantly being revealed to us. One day, He shows Himself through the turbulence of a thunderous storm, *'ino 'ino*, and the next day He brings the soothing gentle rain, *ua*.

If I comb a certain stretch of beach in the morning, then come upon that same spot later in the day, a fresh anticipation fills me. The generous sea may have sent some new cowries or curios since I last visited. Could a piece of brilliant blue sea glass or twisted gray driftwood be waiting for me? Unclaimed treasure awaits discovery.

Similarly, the Scriptures are a source of new revelation every day. While God never changes, He reveals Himself in different ways at different times. He divulges fresh insights to me from His Word, even through passages I thought I knew well.

Even after so many years of following Christ, there are still so many treasures of truth to discover as I seek to know Him more each day.

Today's Treasure

God's greatest gifts are revealed when we take time to look and listen for them.

What facet of God's boundless nature is He revealing to you today?

Snakehead Cowrie

Cypraea caputophidiir

This is the most common cowrie in Hawai'i, and the ones I find most often near my home. They are often found lying on the sand, in shallow water under loose rocks, or lodged in crevices along the shore. Growing up to one inch in length, they are called *leho-kupa* in Hawaiian.

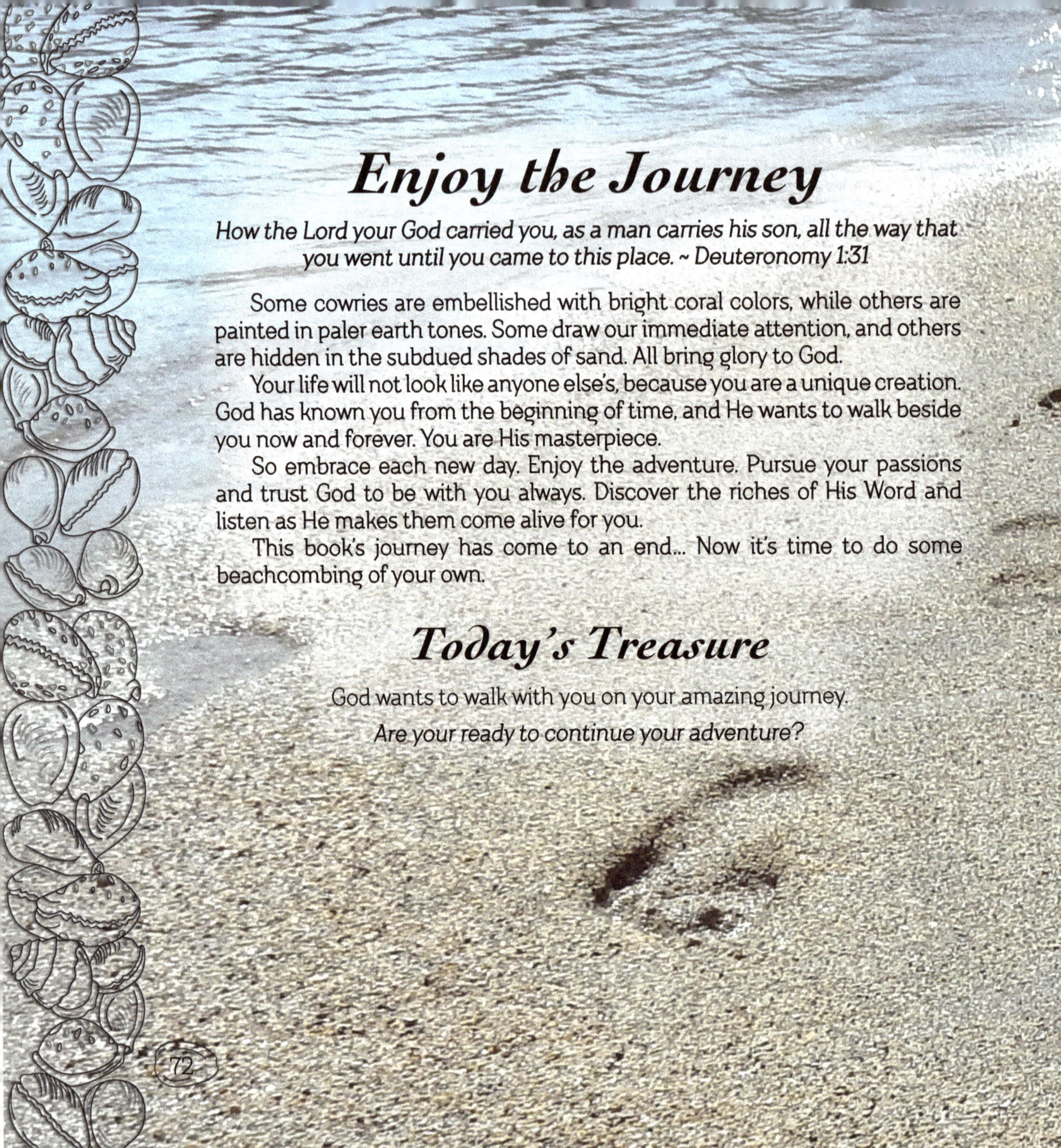

Enjoy the Journey

How the Lord your God carried you, as a man carries his son, all the way that you went until you came to this place. ~ Deuteronomy 1:31

Some cowries are embellished with bright coral colors, while others are painted in paler earth tones. Some draw our immediate attention, and others are hidden in the subdued shades of sand. All bring glory to God.

Your life will not look like anyone else's, because you are a unique creation. God has known you from the beginning of time, and He wants to walk beside you now and forever. You are His masterpiece.

So embrace each new day. Enjoy the adventure. Pursue your passions and trust God to be with you always. Discover the riches of His Word and listen as He makes them come alive for you.

This book's journey has come to an end... Now it's time to do some beachcombing of your own.

Today's Treasure

God wants to walk with you on your amazing journey.

Are your ready to continue your adventure?

73

A Journey for Life

Mahalo for joining me on this journey.

We've stayed the course as we sauntered through joy and rallied through stormy seasons together, all the while uncovering gifts of the sea and truths of the Kingdom.

I hope you keep seeking more of God's treasures as you continue on your God-given path. Notice the small things (like cowrie shells) that are easily passed by. Smell the sea and the sand, the flowers and the grass, the mountains and the trees. Listen to people and take time to really hear them.

And listen for God's voice as He speaks to you through whomever or whatever you may encounter. God is alive and wants to have a relationship with you everyday.

You see, God didn't only lead the Israelites on their journey through the desert. Or the early Hawaiians as they navigated their outriggers across the Pacific headed for undiscovered shores. He is still alive and leading us today. Whether desert, sea, mountain or valley, God is there. We walk by faith, one step at a time, as we listen to the leading of the Holy Spirit.

I'd love to hear from you, too.

Tell me your stories at www.beachwalksandgodtalks.com or beachwalksandgodtalks@gmail.com

Until we meet again, *aloha oe,*

Karen

I love beachcombing.
I love cowrie shells.
I love finding treasure.
I love hearing from God.

And I love sharing these treasures with you...

The Unsurpassable Treasure

For God so loved the world that He gave His only Son, that whoever believes in Him should not perish but have eternal life. ~John 3:16

There is one gift that is greater than all the rest. It is the unsurpassable gift freely given to anyone who puts their faith in Jesus Christ to be their Lord and Savior. A personal relationship with God and eternal life in heaven are yours for the asking.

Jesus spent His life on earth modeling a life of love for us. Then he became the final blood sacrifice when He carried the weight of our sins (wrong things we do) to His death on the cross. When He rose from the grave three days later, He conquered the power of sin and death over us. Later, He rose from the grave and joined His Father in heaven (eternal life), so we could live our lives in the grace of forgiveness.

Even if you were the only person in the world, He would have done this for you. This story of God's love is written in the Holy Bible.

That which is born of the flesh is flesh, and that which is born of the Spirit is spirit. ~John 3:6

Jesus promised He would send us the Holy Spirit when He left this world. It is the Holy Spirit who speaks to our hearts to guide and comfort us. So we have the power of the Trinity of God in Three Persons—Father, Son, and Holy Spirit in this life.

When you ask Jesus to be your Savior and Lord, you become a child of God. You are "born again" in a spiritual sense. As part your inheritance.you are given your own gifts from the Holy Spirit that are richer, deeper and more fulfilling than any treasures the world can offer.

Today's Treasure

Somewhere deep within, we all know there is a part of us that was created to worship God. He is always here, awaiting a seeking heart.

Will you join the family of believers who proclaim together, "Here I am, Lord"?

Mokuaikaua Church

Mokuaikaua Church is known as the first Christian church in the state of Hawai'i. Henry Opukaha'ia's journey to New England as one of the first native Hawaiian Christians influenced fourteen Protestant missionaries to make the almost six-month voyage to Kona, Big Island. Reverend and Mrs. Asa Thurston founded the church in 1820 across from the pier where those first missionaries landed. It is sill the home of a thriving church two hundred years later.

A Lesson in Hawaiian

The Hawaiian language is as beautiful as the islands themselves. Historically, it was an oral tradition until 19th century missionaries put it in written form. If you haven't heard or spoken it before, I hope this short guide will help you get started.

There are only 13 letters in the Hawaiian alphabet, *piapa*, including the 'okina:

A, E, H, I, K, L, M, N, O, P, U, W, '

The 'okina (') is a special symbol in the Hawaiian language. It is used to show a glottal stop similar to the pause made between the syllables of "oh-oh" and adds stress to the marked vowel. It is written as a single open quotation mark. The proper spelling of Hawai'i includes an 'okina.

Most words accent the next to the last syllable and alternate stressing any syllables before that.

W is pronounced the same way as it is in English at the beginning of a word. It usually sounds like v in the middle of a word.

Vowel sounds:

A—as in *about*, or if stressed A—as in *father*
E—as in *get*, or if stressed Ay—as in *bay*
I—as in *party*, or if stressed E—as in *beach*
O—as in *go*
U—as in *lagoon*

Every syllable ends with a vowel. All vowels are pronounced.

Stress the first vowel when vowels are combined.

While this is a simplified guide to pronunciation, you might find it easier to use the phonetic chart I have included with this glossary.

Glossary of Hawaiian Words

HAWAIIAN WORD	PRONUNCIATION	ENGLISH TRANSLATION
'a hui hou kakou	ah-HOO-ee HO-oo kah-KOW	until we meet again
'a'a	ah-AH	a type of rough lava
ahi	AH-hee	fire (or tuna-like fish)
aloha	ah-LOH-ha	hello, goodbye, love, breath
aloha 'aina	ah-LOH-ha ah-EE-nah	love for the land
aloha 'oe	ah-LOH-ha O-ee	farewell to you
anuenue	ah-NOO-eh-NOO-eh	rainbow
ao	ah-OH	daylight
ha	hah	breath of life
Hawai'i nei	ha-VA-ee NAY-ee	this Hawai'i
honu	hoh-NOO	green sea turtle
honua	hoh-NOO-ah	earth
'ino'ino	EE-noh-EE-noh	storm
I'o	EE-oh	the one true God
kahakai	KAH-hah-KAH-ee	beach
kai	KAH-ee	sea water
kahuna	KAH-hoo-NAH	priest
kapu	KAH-poo	law, taboo, prohibited
kau	KAH-oo	season
keiki	KAY-kee	small child

Kona	KOH-nah	district in West Hawai'i
la	lah	sun, day
lanai	lah-NAH-ee	balcony or veranda
lani	LAH-nee	heaven, sky
Lapahoehoe	LAH-pah-HO-ee-HO-ee	town in northeast Hawai'i
leho	LAY-ho	COWRIE shell
lei	LAY-ee	wreath of flowers
mahalo	mah-HAH-loh	thank you
makai	mah-KAH-ee	toward the ocean
makani	mah-KAH-nee	wind
moana	mah-AH-nah	sea
napo'o la	nah-POH-oh-LAH	sunset
ohana	oh-HAH-nah	family, relative
paho'eho'e	pah-HOY-HOY	smooth type of lava
pau	pa-OO or pow	finished, complete, done
piapa	pee-AH-pah	Hawaiian language
pukana la	poo-KAH-nah-LAH	sunrise
pu	poo	Hawaiian conch shell
pule	POO-lay	pray
slippahs	slip-AHS	flip flop sandals, shoes
tsunami	soo-NAH-mee	tidal wave
ua	OO-ah	rain
wai	WAH-ee	fresh water
wana'ao	VAH-nah-AH-oh	dawn

Mahalo Nui Loa

Thank You So Much

"Write down the revelation and make it plain on tablets so that a herald may run with it. For the revelation awaits an appointed time. Though it linger, wait for it; it will certainly come and not delay." ~Habakkuk 2:2–3 NIV

The Lord spoke these verses to me in early 2011. The word *linger* stood out clearly, so I asked God, "How long can something *linger*?"

Evidently, as long as it takes to get to its appointed time. I have learned much during this incubation period, while God added more of His imprint to the pages of this book, as well as to my heart.

Mahalo nui loa isn't a powerful enough expression of my gratitude to the body of Christ who have prayed for me, believed in me, helped me, encouraged me and listened to me since I began writing this at a Christian Writers Conference in Kona, Hawai'i.

Don, you always believed I could and should write this book. Thank you for the unwavering support, love, and encouragement you gave until your last breath. I know how happy you must be to see it finished.

Holly, you were there from the beginning...reading, offering ruthlessly honest feedback, and making sure I stayed true to my "voice" from start to finish.

Also in the beginning, there was the *School of Illustration*, a part of Youth With A Mission in Kona. Big mahalos to all of you, students and staff, who worked on the original concepts even before I began working at the school. *Ava*, you selflessly offered your services by designing the wonderful page borders that can be seen throughout this book. Fellow author, *Lovelle*, you supported me with words of encouragement and invaluable help through the printing process.

Thank you to the writers' groups in Kona and California who provided their feedback and helped me communicate more clearly.

Kathy Ide, you chose my book to win an editing award at the Southern California Christian Writers' Conference, and then turned out to be an outstanding editor, as well as a huge blessing.

Julie Williams, you were the first to catch my vision for this book (which was hard to explain). Over the course of four years, you put to paper what I could only envision in my mind. In the end, we spent hours laying out each page and the book cover via Zoom—while you were in California and I was in Hawai'i. Your opinions and patience were invaluable. You are a godsend and we truly are a "match made in heaven."

Gerry and Del Retta, I could not have done this without you. *Shery*, I loved hearing your input as the finishing touches were being put to press. And to *Patrick Snow*, who coached me through the technical parts of preparing a book for print, mahalo.

This book has been a ten-year journey of discovery, delays, and even death as I pursued the voice of the Holy Spirit. Since I began, both my husband, Don, who was my greatest cheerleader, and my friend, Jennie, who was praying with me that day in 2011, have gone to be with God in heaven. I'd be wrong if I didn't say it's been a long rough road (across fresh 'a'a). But God has been faithful and good. He has seen me through and given me everything and everyone I needed to complete this book in His perfect timing, not my own. Almost as if it was destiny, I finished the inspirational chapters of the book on Pentecost Sunday 2020, which would have been my fortieth wedding anniversary.

Every step of the way, God walked with me. His unfailing love in the hills and the valleys led to a book created in His timing. I hope His imprint is left in your heart as well, as you faithfully listen to His voice and follow His footsteps.

Green Sea Turtle

Green sea turtles, *honu*, are often seen basking on sandy shores or swimming along the shallow waters of Hawai'i. They are native to this land, and get their names from the green fat found beneath their shells. This green color comes from the algae and sea grasses they eat. Honu are the largest hard-shelled turtles in the world, measuring as much as four feet in length and weighing over 300 pounds.

If you are blessed enough to have a honu join you on your swim, you will witness first-hand the gracefulness of this marine marvel. You can check to see if it is a male or a female by looking at its tail. Adult females have shorter tails than adult males. It is recommended that you stay at least ten feet away and refrain from touching this reptile.

Karen of Karmel

Karen Marie Ellison (Karmel) is an author, artist, teacher, and professional speaker living on the Big Island of Hawai'i. Seeing herself as a *painter of life*, she finds inspiration in the artistry of God's creation. Her desire is to share this aloha, *breath of life*, with you.

Her book, cards, and artwork are all part of **Karmel Creations**, an acronym created with the beginning sounds of her full name—KARen Marie ELlison. It also reflects how she was deeply moved by the power of the Holy Spirit at Mount Carmel in Israel, the place where Elijah's God (YHWH) demonstrated His power as the One True God. Finally, her precious mother's middle name was Carmella.

Karen's work is dedicated to the glory of God and is available at:

KarmelCreations.com
and
BeachWalksAndGodTalks.com

If you are interested in having her speak at one of your events, contact her at:

(808) 329-3579 (8:00 AM–5:00 PM HST)
or
BeachWalksAndgGodTalks@gmail.com

"My sheep hear my voice, and I know them, and they follow me." ~John 10:27

Treasures I've Collected on My Journey